Happy Day!

Just as a notice, feel free to print and share this publication with others as long as you include a link back to TheRawAdvantage.com

While in my heart I'd hope all who enjoy and benefit from this book would desire to make a donation, my deepest wish is to simply reach as many people as possible. Without doubt the implementation of these TRA Retreat Treats recipes and concepts, can help bring renewed ease, culinary deliciousness as well as higher levels of health and vitality to all on their path.

Hope to see you at my next retreat!

Happy eating :)

Enjoy much
PeaceLovenSeasonalFruit,

CK

PUBLISHED BY:

Chris Kendall

411 Candle Place
Saskatoon, Sask, Canada
s7k5a8

www.TheRawAdvantage.com

The information and recipes contained within TRA Retreat Treats are neither intended to treat, cure, or diagnose any disease or illness, nor meant to replace your healthcare professional or family physician's advice. As with any major change in diet, it is always recommended to consult your doctor first.

TRA RETREAT TREATS
PREFACE

A self-proclaimed "Nutrition Nerd" since 1998, I obtained certification from an accredited school as a Registered Holistic Nutritionist (RHN) in 2004 and have been a 100% Raw Food Vegan since that time. On my journey of personal growth it has become my greatest joy to be of loving service to others on their path to wellness.

As a registered holistic nutritionist offering 100% raw food and transitional lifestyle coaching, it is my highest hope that you will learn how to increase your wellness in all aspects of your life; from easy weight management, increased athletic performance, enviable well-being, superior resistance to colds and disease (I've had one stress-related sick day in over 14 years) with increased spiritual, mental, and emotional poise. We live in a time where disease of the body and mind is rampant, misinformation is widespread without conscience, and the almighty dollar is above all. I hope to show you how to regain your God-given natural state of pristine health, youthful vitality, and the security of lifelong wellness through improved diet and lifestyle. May you live free and happy without reliance on costly and dangerous pills, drugs, vitamins, "superfoods" or surgery, thriving as nature intended.

-CK

TRA RETREAT TREATS
CONTENTS

THE RAW ADVANTAGE 101 5

TRA RETREAT TREATS 6

WHY RAW 7

FOOD COMBINING 8

ULTIMATE RAW FOOD DISCLAIMER 9

THE TOOLS OF THE TRADE 10

FAVORITE DRINKS* 12

MEXICAN NIGHT* 17

THAI NIGHT* 22

OPEN HOUSE SAMPLERS* 25

ITALIAN NIGHT* 32

MEDITERRANEAN NIGHT* 37

EAST INDIAN NIGHT* 42

FAREWELL BREAKFAST* 47

ABOUT THE CHEFS 51

ABOUT THE RETREAT CENTERS 54

THANKS 57

* Recipes!

TRA RETREAT TREATS
THE RAW ADVANTAGE 101

Welcome and thank you for checking out my TRA Retreat Treats recipe book.

TRA stands for "The Raw Advantage", my baby, my website, my drive, focus, and passion.

I started TheRawAdvantage.com in order to share the life altering changes, benefits, and growth I have experienced, and am continuing to experience, through applying a holistic raw food lifestyle. After 5 years of diet and lifestyle change, while in school to become a RHN, I met Dr. Douglas Graham of **FoodnSport**. At that time Doug was a 25+ Year Raw Foodist. He was the Keynote Speaker at nearly every raw festival with quite a presence. After going to a few of his talks one day, I was blown away and decided to go 100% raw overnight.

Within the first few days of eating raw I experienced a deeper connection to self, more expansive love, bliss, and gratitude for all of creation than at any other time in my life. My path was changed forever. I knew I wanted to learn and experience all I could in the areas of raw foods, self-help/development and fitness. I wanted to do this first, for my own growth, but was really driven even more by my opportunity to help others on their path toward optimal health, fitness, emotional, and spiritual growth.

After 4 years of living the lifestyle, slipping, and at times falling, getting to really know myself through creating ease and growing through acceptance, I launched **TheRawAdvantage.com** in late 2008. With my website up and running I starting by sharing tips, tricks, inspiration, and recipes, then videos, all aimed to help bring common sense, fun and ease to a holistic raw food lifestyle. The last few years has seen me chef-ing large festivals and retreats such as the **Woodstock Fruit Festival**, my own retreats, as well as providing consultations; in person, phone, Skype, and as a live in lifestyle coach.

For the last 5 years I've been continually flowing and growing in my passions and feel blessed living my dream through helping others in loving service.

A huge turn in 2012 sprouting the TRAdream, A Non Profit aimed at creating fully by donation raw food retreat/learning centers around the world. At this Point TRAdream is Incorporated in Washington, is a full on Registered Non-Profit and we are seeking 501(c)(3) charity status.

It's my belief that we all have everything we need. That perfection is inherent in the process, and that it's through sharing that which we are abundant, in that everyone comes to know the truth of abundance.

Learn more about TRA dream at TheRawAdvantage.com!

TRA RETREAT TREATS

At the Turn of Dec 2012, I teamed up with Megan Elizabeth McDonnell to smash out two epic retreats!

In the transformational and hyped up times of mid December 2012 Megan and I ventured into Mexico, Valladolid to be exact. The mission to help open my friends Beate n Paul Epp's new 811 raw food bed and breakfast, with a Bang! The retreat took place at their brand new dream, **Casa Axis Mundi**, and was dubbed "Gateway to the Golden Age" a culinary/transformative retreat. The focus was on making raw food prep / culinary creation fun, simple, and easy while delving into the deeper emotional and social aspects of raw that come up with such lifestyle changes. Beyond raw food prep, amazing sharing sessions and talks, we also went to the most amazing white sand beaches, visited some Mayan ruins, and went to amazing Cenote's (natural Underground Caves and Swimming Holes) explored farmers markets, and beautiful small city sites. All I can say is amazing amazing amazing!

Our next retreat Mission had us heading to visit my 2nd Family, Brian and Jody Calvi at The **Farm of Life** in Costa Rica, a most epic raw food healing retreat center and organic farm. There, we set out to smash a more adventuresome raw food, yoga, surfing, and skateboarding retreat. The Farm of Life is truly an amazing holistic healing retreat center that teaches equal focus on all aspects of health, from emotional poise, exercise, sunbathing, sun gazing, natural spring water, a simple raw diet, and more. All activities optional from epic waterfalls, breathtaking jungle hikes, Kendalini and raw power yoga, amazing world class surfing, great skateboarding, 4 Cravings Busters recipes/food demos, not to mention all the organic raw fruits and vegetables one could eat... Seriously it's hard to have a better time.

It's so hard to put these experiences into words, short of you coming to my next retreat... Hint hint. Since you weren't at either of these retreats I feel I can do you the most justice by creating this book, sharing the rawsome culinary creations, pictures, hints and vibes from those amazing times. I really hope you love, love, love these recipes, They were handpicked by the retreat attendees and created from some of Megan Elizabeth McDonnell, Beate Epp and my own favorite raw recipes. I see this as a perfect Segway between my Simple Hygienic 811 RV **101 Frickin' Rawsome Recipes** and my upcoming "Cravings Busters, Transitional Raw Gourmet" Book Series.

So excited for many more fun retreats to come, hope to grow with you at one!

Learn more about the retreats at TheRawAdvantage.com!

TRA RETREAT TREATS
WHY RAW

When asked "Does a raw food diet work..." I can't help but smile seeing a huge opportunity to share potent information.

Each and every species on the planet has a species specific diet. I find it hard to believe we are the exception. Virtually each and every living being on the planet lives and thrives off of a 100% raw food diet, that is unless they are fed by humans or scavenge off of us. Think about it, from cows, to frogs, birds, whales, snails, snakes, tree's as well as our closest genetic relatives, the bonobo (a pigmy chimpanzee) they all live and thrive on a 100% raw food diet. All animals eat the foods they can easily catch/gather/bite without the use of any tools or processing of any kind. A neat side note, on average the strongest, least aggressive, and longest lived animals tend to be plant eaters!

Looking to comparative anatomy we are classified as fruigivores, just the same as are our closest living relatives the bonobo or pigmy chimpanzee. As far as DNA goes human males are closer genetically to male bonobo's than to human females. What do bonobos eat? A diet rich in whole fresh fruits, greens and tender young shoots. In fact the bonobo eats more fruit than any of the primates and are markedly the most intelligent as well as peaceful of all apes and monkeys.

Each and every cell in our body requires high quality water, our digestive system requires fiber for digestive functions, all of our tissues require micro nutrients in the form of vitamins, minerals, antioxidants Etc., and macro nutrient in the form of amino acids, fats (EFA's), and carbohydrates. Easy to digest raw fruits and tender young leafy green vegetables meet all of our food born nutrient needs so closely that they are always our number 1 or number 2 choice for health calorie per calorie.

Some may argue that primates are not vegan, That some insects and at times low incidence of animal foods are in their diet. Interestingly enough when given adequate quantities of fruit bonobos will eat solely of plant foods. The Academy of Nutrition and Dietetics has gone on record saying "planned vegetarian diets, including total vegetarian or vegan diets, are healthful, nutritionally adequate, and may provide health benefits in the prevention and treatment of certain diseases." [eatright.org].

We can go further than that when we come to know these truths experientially. I Say Let your own intuition and Experience be the Guide, Learn from those with the qualities and Results you're looking for.

Enjoy the sweet side of life!

TRA RETREAT TREATS
FOOD COMBINING

Food combining has brought me so much benefit I wish to give you a basic intro as it applies to this recipe book.

A side note, in 101 Frickin Rawsome Recipes, the aim was to share "perfect" or "proper" food combining. This book tends to bend the "rules" or, as I say "tools", at times, say for "Cravings Busters" or special occasion meals. I find it's important to note that the ratios of the ingredients in any combination make a big difference in food combining. For example (see Tip 2 below), a 50/50 mixture of date and tomato would create lots of digestive discomfort, bubbles, burps, and farts, while a few dates in a liter or two of tomato sauce may go unnoticed. Quantity makes a big difference.

Digestion is much more complicated than many of us notice and can easily be explained through physiology and chemistry. Certain foods digest well together while others do not, this is due to the nature of the food itself. Each foods individual transit time as well as the different mediums, stages, and digestive juices the body uses to break down different foods affect the digestive process.

Most of us have made a habit since an early age to eat all types of foods together, this is not our natural behavior, nor the behavior of animals in the wild. When you watch any animal/insect/reptile in nature, one may notice, they eat the foods they are physiologically designed for, one at a time, most often exclusively until full. While one food at a time is optimal for digestion, it is understandable that we desire variety, this can be accomplished through proper food combining.

I most definitely am not laying down a set of rules here, these are simply time tested and proven tools that can help you day by day and meal by meal. Really it's what you do most often that will have the most pronounced effects. If you wish to experience excellent digestion, near odorless quick and easy elimination, unrivalled nutrient absorption, and receive the surplus of energy that comes from streamlining your bodies energy expenditures, test for yourself, eat more mono meals, and I dare ya to try out these guidelines:

TIP 1: All Fresh Ripe Raw fruits digest best on a fully empty stomach. EAT FRUIT FIRST.

TIP 2: Sweet fruit does not digest well with acid fruit, e.g. bananas and oranges, lemons and dates etc.

TIP 3: Fatty foods do not mix well with sweet fruits except in small quantities (e.g. Durian)

TIP 4: Acidic fruits combine well with fats (e.g. tomato or citrus with avocado or nuts)

TIP 5: Lettuce and celery/young tender leafy greens combine well with everything.

TRA RETREAT TREATS
ULTIMATE RAW FOOD DISCLAIMER

Each and every piece of whole, fresh, ripe, raw produce tastes different, even if from the same tree! The taste as well as the water-content of fruits and vegetables can vary dependent on the soil they were grown, the actual variety, elevation, weather, sun exposure, general growing methods and even intention of the grower. Going even further recipe likes and dislikes vary dependent upon individuals personal taste..

With this I am encouraging the Creator in you to be..

Well, flexible and creative. When making a dish, taste each ingredient. Use more of the ones that taste really good and/or substitute for other ingredients that really "pop", simple right?

If a sauce ends up runny or too dry adjust using dehydrated ingredients or thin with more of the watery ones, kapeesh?

In the end this is simply asking you to be consciously creative in the moment, adding aliveness and your own flair in the kitchen, seeing recipes as a guide.

As a note unless otherwise specified all recipes are approximate for one serving.

Happy creating!

TRA RETREAT TREATS
TOOLS OF THE TRADE
RAW FOOD PREP APPLIANCES

A GOOD BLENDER:

The Almightily Vitamix. I highly recommend that anyone serious about his or her health invest in a Vitamix. It is without a doubt the best blender and most useful tool for both the new and seasoned raw foodist. Any texture can be effortlessly achieved while making green smoothies, sauces, soups, stews, nut butters, dips and ice creams, in any quantity you choose. After owning one for over 11 years, often using it as much as three times a day, travelling with it, lending it to family and friends, repeatedly recommending many others to purchase one, I decided to become a Vitamix affiliate. With all honesty I feel my Vitamix is the best investment I have ever made in my health. I recommend it as a first priority in taking steps to increase your overall percentage of raw food consumption and changing your lifestyle for the better.

You can order your very own **Vitamix** at TheRawAdvantage.com.

* Free shipping to Canada and the US!
  Use my affiliate code: 06-004171

SHREDDERS, SLICERS AND NOODLE MAKERS:

There are a variety of tools with which to slice, dice and make noodles out of fruits and vegetables. Most often a simple knife will suffice, but using tools can make the job faster, more uniform, and provide a change in the taste, appearance, and texture of a meal. A simple grater can be used normally for slaws, or to make noodles by grating the vegetable carefully lengthways along the notches. A regular carrot peeler can typically make neat, thick, flat noodles out of almost any veggie or fruit. My favorite handheld tool is a specialty peeler with small blades that makes excellent linguini noodles. Most often this type of tool is called a "julienne peeler" and I have seen

TRA RETREAT TREATS
TOOLS OF THE TRADE

these at many a department and kitchen stores.

There is also the trusty mandolin, if you feel comfortable using one, which can easily make a variety of slices and noodles.

That said, I am so stoked to offer the Amazing Joyce Chen Spiral Slicer, also known as the Saladacco Spiralizer. Having tried many noodle makers, I think this is by far the best. This tool easily and quickly produces the thinnest most tender angel hair pasta noodles of any device. Anyone can make amazing raw dishes that really brings to life the taste and texture of traditional pasta. You can use zucchini, carrots, beets, hardier squash, cucumber, celeriac or any other root veggie to create the lightest, most delicious, nutritious noodles and the most eye-popping presentation possible.

Get your Joyce Chen Spiral Slicer at TheRawAdvantage.com!

DEHYDRATOR:

While fresh food is typically best, using a dehydrator can help create new textures, enhance taste, and bring warmth to raw meals at those Cravings Busters times. From wraps, stir fries, pancakes, crepes, homemade spices and thickeners, to travel food and saving or storing extra produce, or simply to gently warm up a dish, the dehydrator can be proven indispensable. While some of the recipes within Cravings Busters use the dehydrator, others do not. I recommend only a small part of any meal being dehydrated, and even then, only partially so.

Having researched and used more than a few dehydrators at home and at raw festivals, retreats, and events, I without doubt find the Excalibur to be of the highest quality and consistency for the best price. As an affiliate I am able to bring you this awesome dehydrator at the best possible price.

Order your **Excalibur Dehydrator** with free shipping at TheRawAdvantage.com

TRA RETREAT TREATS
DRINKS & SMOOTHIES

CHOCOLATE MONKEY LAVA

WATERMELON PP

RASPBERRY-VANILLA SMOOTHIE

BERRY PUDDING PIE SMOOTHIE

TRA RETREAT TREATS
CHOCOLATE MONKEY LAVA

I love love love my Chocolate Monkey recipe from '101 Frickin' Rawsome Recipes', honestly I make it nonstop! This is a tweaked version of it I got hinted to from my Friend Lisa Sobolewski of **Just Food** while out at the **Farm of Life** in Costa Rica. I'll admit, at the time I didn't want to like it, because of the lava... But it's a hit with most and something I now love making on occasion for a lava kick.

INGREDIENTS:

8 - 16 cavendish Bananas
1 - 3 tbs raw Carob powder
Water, to desired consistency
Hot Pepper, to taste

PREPARATION:

Peel as many bananas as it takes for you to feel like a Banana Commander, place them in the blender. Add carob powder, the hot pepper and if water to desired consistency, I often make with no water or just a cup. Blend, blend, blend, and enjoy the Chocolate Banana Lava!

TRA RETREAT TREATS
WATERMELON PP

I just had to! This is a really refreshing drink that may just get you so hydrated you need to go PP. An instant favorite with the Costa Rica crew, you can serve this as a juice or a smoothie. Mix in a 50/50 ratio...

INGREDIENTS:

Watermelon, as much as your bladder can handle!
Pineapple, equal amount by weight
Peppermint, to taste

PREPARATION:

This is as simple as can be, Watermelon PP! If your using seedless watermelon simply blend equal parts melon and pineapple with the peppermint then either strain with a nutmilk bag or cheese cloth and serve as a juice or leave as is and serve as a smoothie. If using seeded melon blend this first with the mint and strain then add the pineapple for a smoothie, or blend all together and strain for a juice. Whoa confusing but so so simple and amazing!! Enjoy it!

TRA RETREAT TREATS
RASPBERRY-VANILLA SMOOTHIE
BY MEGAN ELIZABETH

Milkshakes and ice cream used to be two of my favorite entertainment and comfort foods. It's amazing to be able to recreate a healthy guilt-free version of a vanilla milkshake, and add a bit of a twist with frozen berries!

INGREDIENTS:

6 Bananas (fresh or frozen)
4 Dates, de-pitted
1 cup Raspberries
1 ½ cups Water or Coconut Water
1 tsp shredded Coconut
½ tsp Vanilla extract

PREPARATION:

If you're using a high speed blender and you feel confident that your blender can power through everything, then add all of the ingredients into the blender and blend until it's evenly mixed. Otherwise, if you are not using a high speed blender, soak your dates ahead of time in water for about 15 to 20 minutes. To make sure your smoothie is extra smooth, you can blend the dates with the raspberries and water first, then blend in the bananas and the rest of the ingredients and blend all together for desired consistency.

TRA RETREAT TREATS
BERRY PUDDING PIE SMOOTHIE
BY MEGAN ELIZABETH

Date smoothies have become very popular among low-fat raw vegans because they are quick, easy, and delicious fuel. This smoothie puts a spin on a LFRV favorite and lends a bit of variety with frozen fruit and lemon. You can try it with a mixture of berries or just chose your favorite one.

INGREDIENTS:

14 medjool Dates
2 cups mixed Berries (frozen)
2 cups Water
1 tbs fresh Lemon juice

PREPARATION:

For this recipe you will want to soak the dates for 20 to 30 minutes in water regardless of whether you are using a high speed or lower speed blender. Then just add everything to the blender and go! Blend, I mean! Go blend!

TRA RETREAT TREATS
MEXICAN NIGHT

SIMPLE SALSA

GREAT GUACAMOLE

CHIPS N RICE

WONDERFUL WRAPS

TRA RETREAT TREATS
SIMPLE SALSA

As the name suggests this is a really basic salsa great for any occasion, even a base recipe. Enjoy with wraps, Chips, Salads, or as a base for a soup!

INGREDIENTS:

6 roma Tomatoes
½ - 1 bunch Cilantro
3 Green Onions
3 Dates or 1 Mango
1 Lime

OPTIONAL:
¼ Pineapple
¼ cup Sun-Dried Tomatoes
Hot Pepper, to taste

PREPARATION:

Cut the top ¼ off of the tomatoes (stem end) and put aside. Dice all of the remaining tomatoes (and optional pineapple to taste) and place in a bowl. Finely chop the cilantro and tops of the green onion and mix in with the tomatoes. Blend the tops of the tomatoes with the bottom of the green onion, lime, dates or mango to taste and add optional sun dried tomatoes and hot pepper. Blend till smooth adjusting amounts to flavor and taste. Pour over diced ingredients and mix well. I like it thick n spicy. Enjoy playing with this…

TRA RETREAT TREATS
GREAT GUACAMOLE

Who doesn't like creamy rich Guacamole? This is a simple and great classic recipe.

INGREDIENTS:
1 - 2 roma Tomatoes
½ - 1 Avocado
¼ - ½ bunch Cilantro
1 - 2 Green Onions
1 - 2 Lime

OPTIONAL:
¼ Pineapple
¼ cup Sun-Dried Tomatoes
Hot Pepper, to taste

PREPARATION:
Cut the top ¼ off of the tomatoes (stem end) and put aside. Dice all of the remaining tomatoes (and optional pineapple to taste) and place in a bowl. Finely chop the cilantro and tops of the green onion and mix in with the tomatoes. Blend the tops of the tomatoes with the bottom of the green onion, lime, dates or mango to taste and add optional sun dried tomatoes and hot pepper. Blend till smooth adjusting amounts to flavor and taste. Pour over diced ingredients and mix well. I like it thick n spicy. Enjoy playing with this...

TRA RETREAT TREATS
CHIPS N' RICE

Jicama is a really great ingredient for making chips and rice, enjoy them when you can find them. Rice can be made with many other ingredients such as cauliflower, hear of palm, parsnips, daikon, and coconut etc.

INGREDIENTS:
1 - 2 Jicama

OPTIONAL:
Cauliflower
Chives

PREPARATION:
Peel and slice very thinly, 1/6 " for chips and serve. Alternately one can squeeze lime on top and dehydrate until dry. Beware: it will shrink a ton! For rice, peel jicama, grate with a fine grater then lightly pulse in a food processor till desired "rice" size and look. Squeeze all liquid out for a lighter fluffier taste, look and feel. Serve with wraps, on its own or as a base layer for salsa n guacamole, or curries, etc.

TRA RETREAT TREATS
WONDERFUL WRAPS

Wraps are such a great hand held treat, so many varieties available this is one of the simplest yet tasty raw wraps.

INGREDIENTS:

2 - 3 Collard Leaves (or Romaine, Iceburg, Nappa, etc)
Salsa (recipe above)
Guacamole (recipe above)
Sprouts (your favourite kind)
Rice (recipe above)
Hot Sauce (to taste)

PREPARATION:

Select big collard green leaves (or other big leaves), De-stem by cutting at the base and following the central vein up the leaf with a paring knife. Careful not to cut the leaf, just remove the leaf stem. Fill first with "rice" then salsa, guacamole, sprouts, and hot sauce. Make hot sauce by blending the extra liquid from salsa with a bit of extra lime, a date, hot pepper, green onion and sun dried tomato to desired taste and consistency. Enjoy!!

TRA RETREAT TREATS
THAI NIGHT

COCONUT CURRY NOODLE SALAD

COCONUT CURRY SAUCE

TRA RETREAT TREATS
COCONUT CURRY NOODLE SALAD

I absolutely love all Thai Dishes especially coconut noodle dishes. This simple recipe is so so tasty and easy to digest I love to share it and eat it whenever desired.

INGREDIENTS:

¼ head Nappa Cabbage
1 medium Zucchini
4 -6 large stems Bok Choy
⅛ head Red Cabbage
½ Red Pepper
4 Mushrooms (shitake or crimini)

OPTIONAL:
2 cups Bean Sprouts
Daikon Radish, to taste

PREPARATION:

Slice the napa and red cabbage thin like noodles and chop the bok choy. Using a mandolin or julienne peeler make noodles out of zucchini and optional daikon (reserving bits). Dice tops of green onions, Slice mushrooms, julienne red pepper add optional bean sprouts and mix. Set aside and make sauce.

TRA RETREAT TREATS
COCONUT CURRY SAUCE

The secret to a great dish imho is a great sauce, coconuts make an amazing base for countless sauces. This is one of my favorite basic thai curry sauces, I really hope you love it.

INGREDIENTS:

(All salad trimmings can be reserved for the sauce)

1 brown Coconut

2 - 3 stalks Celery

1 Carrot

1 - 3 Dates

2 - 3 Green Onions

1 bunch of Thai basil or basil

1 - 2 tablespoons Tamarind (or Apricot, or Lime)

2 - 4 Sun-Dried Tomatoes

OPTIONAL:

Ginger

Garlic

Hot pepper

PREPARATION:

Pop a hole in the top of the old coconut, drain liquid into vitamix container and break open shell. Using a spoon or carefully a knife remove insides from shell and add to blender (if you don't have a vitamix you will need grate the coconut). You will only need half the water and coconut, cover and put away half or make tons of sauce and keep extra. Roughly cut carrots and celery and add to container with coconut water and optional ginger. Blend till smooth using the tamper with gusto at high speed. Strain through a nut milk bag or cheese cloth into a bowl and then pour back in the blender. Add 2 dates, green onions, bits from zucchini/daikon, 2 - 4+ sun dried tomatoes, a few tablespoons of tamarind and optional garlic/ginger/hot pepper, Blend well. If you need it thicker consider adding more sun dried tomatoes, dried zucchini, dried pineapple or a small handful of favourite seeds.

Mix over noodles and enjoy!

TRA RETREAT TREATS
OPEN HOUSE SAMPLERS

MUSHROOM STUFFERS

CUCUMBER SLIDERS

SAVORY AVOCADO DRESSING

PIZZA BITES

PERFECT PORTOBELLO CAP PIZZAS

SPINACH SOUP

TRA RETREAT TREATS
MUSHROOM STUFFERS

Amazing bite sized mushroom stuffers, packed with earthy creamy n savory flavors, sure to leave you wanting more each bite. Go ahead make a few trays!

INGREDIENTS:

Button, Crimini and/or Portobello Mushrooms
1 Lime

FILLING:
1 young Thai Coconut jelly
1 cup Coconut Water
¼ cup Pecans
¼ cup Green Onion, chopped
1 heaping tablespoon fresh Rosemary, chopped
juice of ½ Lemon

PREPARATION:

Pop all the stems off the mushrooms and place them on the dehydrator trays. Squeeze a little bit of lime inside each of the mushrooms. Set the dehydrator to 109 degrees and dehydrate for 2 to 4 hours or until the mushrooms are tender. On a sunny day you can can also leave the mushrooms in the sun for 2 to 4 hours so they can marinate, soften, and soaked up some Vitamin D. Make the filling while the mushrooms are dehydrating. Add all the filling ingredients into the blender and blend it until it's smooth and evenly mixed. When the mushrooms have been in the dehydrator for around 2 hours add the filing and place them back in for another 2 hours. You can garnish each mushrooms with chopped green onion and/or red pepper.

TRA RETREAT TREATS
CUCUMBER SLIDERS
BY MEGAN ELIZABETH

Everyone who tries this dish is always pleasantly surprised. It is one of the easiest raw snacks to prepare and not only does it look appetizing, but the taste is flavorful and refreshing.

INGREDIENTS:

1 Cucumber, sliced into 16 pieces
16 slices of Tomato (about 2 - 3 Roma Tomatoes)
16 pieces fresh Dill, Basil, Mint, or Cilantro
4 Medjool Dates, quartered

PREPARATION:

On top of cucumber, layer tomato, then date, and finally the herb of choice.

TRA RETREAT TREATS
SAVORY AVOCADO DRESSING
BY MEGAN ELIZABETH

I initially made this salad dressing in Hawaii because the avocados were so amazing I found myself using avocado more than usual. It became a staple salad dressing for me and I made it at least once or twice a week.

INGREDIENTS:

1 cup of fresh squeezed Orange juice
½ Avocado
¼ cup chopped Green Onion
¼ cup Cilantro (more if you like)
4 - 6 leaves of Mint

PREPARATION:

Add all the ingredients to the blender. Blend until it's smooth and evenly mixed. Pour over a super huge yummy salad with romaine or baby romaine lettuce, chopped tomatoes, and chopped zucchini.

TRA RETREAT TREATS
PIZZA BITES

Who doesn't Love Pizza? I love love love Pizza Bites even more! Having served full dinners of pizza bites, enjoying many different variations, I find everyone, including me, is always wishing for just a few more.

INGREDIENTS:

1 - 2 Zucchini
4 - 6 Tomatoes
¼ cup Sun-Dried Tomatoes
2 Green Onions
½ bunch Basil
small handful Oregano
1 Red Bell Pepper
5 Mushroom
2 Dates

OPTIONAL:
Garlic, to taste
Pineapple
Hot Pepper, to taste

PREPARATION:

Slice tomatoes and dehydrate at 109° for 4 hours, 2 hours later peel zucchini and slice into ¼" rounds, place on a dehydrator tray for 2 hours at 109°, or in the sun, till just softened. Blend partially dried tomatoes with bottoms of the green onion, oregano (this is the secret to pizza sauce) ¼ of the red pepper, dates and optional ingredients. Pulse in half of the basil, slowly (basil loses its flavor if over blended). Slice the mushrooms thin. Fine dice the remaining red pepper and green onion tops into a confetti. Top each zucchini round with a leaf of basil, then a spoon of pizza sauce, followed by confetti and mushroom and/or pineapple; endless variations. Add back to the dehydrator for 1-2 more hours at 109° to warm and intensify the flavor.

Note: this can be done without dehydrating, simply use more sun dried tomatoes in the sauce.

TRA RETREAT TREATS
PERFECT PORTOBELLO CAP PIZZAS

The name really says it all, these are perfect. With the intensified flavor explosion, amazing texture and satisfying quality these bring you may start with one but by the time you are finished you will wish you had made more. A definite crowd favorite.

INGREDIENTS:

Portobello Mushrooms, 1 cap per person
Roma Tomatoes, 1 - 2 per person
2 Green Onions
½ cup Sun-Dried Tomatoes
½ bunch Basil
small handful Oregano
1 Red Pepper
2 Dates
Lime

OPTIONAL:
Garlic, to taste
Pineapple
Hot Pepper, to taste

PREPARATION:

Slice tomatoes and Pull stems off Mushrooms, squeeze lime on Mushrooms and dehydrate both at 109° for 4 hours. At 2 hours peel tomatoes off and blend Most partially dried tomatoes with bottoms of the green onion, oregano (this is the secret to pizza sauce) ¼ of the red pepper, dates and optional ingredients. Pulse in half of the basil, slowly (basil loses its flavor if over blended). Slice the mushrooms thin. Fine dice the remaining red pepper and green onion tops into a confetti. Top each zucchini round with a leaf of basil, then a spoon of pizza sauce, followed by confetti and mushroom and/or pineapple; endless variations. Add back to the dehydrator for 1-2 more hours at 109° to warm and intensify the flavor.

Note: this can be done without dehydrating, simply use more sun dried tomatoes in the sauce.

TRA RETREAT TREATS
SPINACH SOUP
BY BEATE EPP

A subtle update to Beate Epp's delicious spinach soup, enjoyed by all at the Casa Axis Mundi open house!

INGREDIENTS:

2 cups young Thai Coconut Water (1.5 - 2 Coconuts)
1 large bunch Spinach
1 - 2 bunches Cilantro
4 stalks Celery
2 Green Onions
2 Medjool Dates

OPTIONAL:
½ - 1 Jalapeño Pepper
dash of Cumin

PREPARATION:

Open young coconut(s) and pour the water into your blender. If necessary open a second coconut. Add spinach, cilantro, celery, green onions, dates and optional ingredients if you dare. Blend till smooth (or chunky) adding more coconut water if thinner soup is desired. Super delicious!! I like it with a whole jalapeño kick!

TRA RETREAT TREATS
ITALIAN NIGHT

CHUNKY TOMATO SAUCE

CREAMY ALFREDO SAUCE

TOMATO SOUP

COCO BUTTER ASPARAGUS

TRA RETREAT TREATS
CHUNKY TOMATO SAUCE

I love love love zucchini noodles, or rather I love them more with the perfect sauce, and this is one of those. Thick, hearty, and nostalgia-inducing, this sauce will leave you eating plate after plate without that heavy pasta feeling.

INGREDIENTS:

5-8 Roma Tomatoes
½ head Cauliflower
1 cup Sun-Dried Tomatoes
2 - 3 Dates (or Mango)
2 Green Onions
1 small bunch of Basil
Oregano/Arugula, to taste

OPTIONAL:
Garlic
Cumin

PREPARATION:

If you have a dehydrator, slice ¾ of the tomatoes into ¼" slices and dehydrate for 4-6 hours at 109°. If you do not have a dehydrator, you should use 2-3x more sun dried tomatoes to thicken the sauce. Dice the last ¼ of tomatoes, chop green onion tops and place both in a big bowl. Blend partially dehydrated tomatoes (or fresh) with sun dried tomatoes, dates, oregano and if desired, optional ingredients. This should be really thick, add more sun dried tomatoes if needed. Add cauliflower, basil and any zucchini bits from your zucchini pasta (usually 2 medium zucchini per person), pulse lightly (not over 5-6 on vitamix) using tamper to push bits into the blades. Pour over chunks and mix well. Serve over zucchini noodles or anything you like!

CREAMY ALFREDO SAUCE

TRA RETREAT TREATS
BY MEGAN ELIZABETH

Who doesn't love alfredo? Creamy, warm pasta with fresh herbs is the ultimate comfort food. Enjoy this one guilt-free!

INGREDIENTS:

1 young Thai Coconut jelly
1 cup Coconut Water
¼ cup Hemp Seeds
¼ cup Green Onion, chopped
1 heaping tablespoon fresh Rosemary, chopped
1 teaspoon Oregano
¼ cup Cilantro
½ Lemon, juiced

PREPARATION:

Add all the ingredients to the blender and blend until it's smooth and evenly mixed. Have a little extra coconut water or water handy in case you need to thin out the sauce a bit and add it as needed. Pour over zucchini pasta and immediately devour it all by yourself! Just kidding, share share share the deliciousness!

TRA RETREAT TREATS
TOMATO SOUP

I love love love tomatoes. Can you tell? This simple tomato soup can be made quickly and always is a huge crowd-pleaser. I prefer to use heirlooms or early girl tomato's but any sweet and juicy tomato works well. This recipe is based off a 70/30 ratio of tomato to mango, enjoy other ratios for different flavors.

INGREDIENTS:

Tomatoes, 6 - 8 heirloom (or double quantity of Early Girl or Campri)
¼ cup Sun-Dried Tomatoes
1-2 medium Mango
1 Green Onions
1 bunch of Basil
Arugula, to taste
Lime, to taste

OPTIONAL:
Hot Pepper

PREPARATION:

Slice the bottom ⅔ of the top off the tomato, just leaving the smaller end as the bottom. Dice this smaller section and place in a nice bowl, cut the larger end (stem end) in half and add to the blender. Peel and squeeze the mango's into the blender (plant the pit!) and add the bottom of the green onions and optional hot pepper. Blend well. Add the Sun-Dried tomatoes, green onion greens, cilantro, arugula and lime. Pulse blend into desired consistency. I like it a bit chunky. Taste, add ingredients to adjust flavor if necessary, then pour over the bowl of diced tomatoes! Enjoy a ton!

TRA RETREAT TREATS
COCO BUTTER ASPARAGUS

I used to love buttered asparagus, mixed with garlic and hot sauce... Well I discovered a way to have it raw vegan style. With the optional ingredients or not, dehydrated or not, these can pack a mean punch!

INGREDIENTS:

1 young Thai Coconut jelly
Asparagus, 8 - 12
2 ½-inch stalk Celery
Tomato, juice squeezed from ½ a Roma)
1 - 2 Green onions

OPTIONAL:
½ - 1 Jalapeño
½ clove Garlic

PREPARATION:

Snap hard bottoms off asparagus and place in a flat glass dish. Scoop young jelly into blender (should be near clear or thin n white), Blend with celery, white of onion, juice of tomato (eat rest) and optional garlic/pepper. Pour over asparagus and let marinate and/or dehydrate 109°-114° (in same dish) for 1-3 hours or desired texture.

TRA RETREAT TREATS
MEDITERRANEAN NIGHT

TERRIFIC TABOULI

TANGY TZATZIKI SAUCE

BEST FALAFEL BALLS

FRICKIN' FALAFELS

TRA RETREAT TREATS
TERRIFIC TABOULI

If you're really going for a mediterranean night, tabouli is a must! A little more hearty than a regular salad, filled to the brim with delicious flavors this version offers a nice fat free kick!

INGREDIENTS:

⅓ medium Cauliflower
1 roma Tomato
½ red Pepper
¼ cup Red Cabbage, shredded
¼ bunch Cilantro
¼ bunch Parsley
4 Green Onions
½ Cucumber
½ Lemon
½ Mango

OPTIONAL
dash of Cumin

PREPARATION:

Chop and pulse cauliflower in a food processor until resembles "couscous" pill like texture. Alternately simply finely shave off the florets of 1 cauliflower, makes a "couscous like" texture. Remove insides of tomato, place in blender and dice the rest adding to cauliflower. Dice red pepper, cucumber (removing seeds and placing in blender) shred cabbage and herbs. Blend tomato insides with cucumber insides, lemon, mango and optional Ingredient, if desired, till smooth. Mix well with tabouli mixture and let sit to marinate 1/2 hour. Mix and serve with falafel or in a cabbage leaf itself!

HOT TIP:
½ an avocado cubed and stirred in can cream up and add depth to this dish.

TRA RETREAT TREATS
TANGY TZATZIKI SAUCE

A nice creamy and tangy tzatziki sauce makes a falafel go from good to Great!! Simple and quick as can be this recipe is Best made ½ hour in advance for the flavors to mingle and set in.

INGREDIENTS:

½ Zucchini, peeled
½ Cucumber, peeled
¼ cup young Thai Coconut jelly
1 Lemons
2 Sun-Dried Tomatoes halves
Mint and/or Dill, to taste

OPTIONAL:
1 clove Garlic
1 teaspoon Cumin

PREPARATION:

Peel and blend zucchini with the seeds of the cucumber, the young coconut jelly, juice of the lemon, sun dried tomatoes and optional garlic. Lightly pulse in the cucumber and herbs leaving small bits for texture. Serve over falafel, for a falafel salad or cucumbers.

HOT TIP:
Subtitute the coconut jelly for raw sesame seeds for a change.

TRA RETREAT TREATS
BEST FALAFEL BALLS

What are falafels without the perfect crispy falafel ball? Texture and taste is key. After trying more than a few recipes, I really feel I nailed it! This recipe is fairly easy to make, tastes just like the real thing, and leaves you feeling light! Makes 6-10 balls.

INGREDIENTS:

DRY

⅓ medium Cauliflower
¼ cup raw Walnuts
½ medium Carrot
½ medium Zucchini
2 Green Onions
Cilantro, Oregano, and Parsley, to taste

WET

½ medium Zucchini
⅙ cup dry Chickpeas (Soaked 12 hours, sprouted 6 - 8)
1 Lemon
¼ small Red Onion
1 small handful raw Pumpkin Seeds

OPTIONAL

Garlic
1 tsp Cumin

PREPARATION:

Fine-grate and loosely chop the cauliflower, walnuts, carrot and zucchini from the dry ingredients. Mix well. Finely chop the green onions and herbs to taste, mix together. Peel zucchini in the wet list, blend with chickpeas (should be soaked 12 hours, drained and let sit with 1 rinse 6-8 hours. Will double in size), juiced lemon, red onion, pumpkin seeds and optional ingredients (recommended). Pour wet ingredients over dry, mix really well. Should be thick and slightly wet. Form into small golf ball sized falafels, squeeze hard enough ftp form solid balls or just a tiny bit of juice to come out. Place on dehydrator trays (I recommend Excalibur) and dehydrate for 6-8 hours at 115° turning over once half way. Balls should be crisp on the outside, slightly moist in the middle.

Serve warm on a salad or in the beautiful Frickin' Falafel recipe (below) Double, triple, quadruple the recipe and freeze for up to a few months for future Frickin Falafels, or maybe a falafel party! Serious stuff. ;) Play with size and dehydration time for texture. Enjoy!

TRA RETREAT TREATS
FRICKIN' FALAFELS

During my vegetarian days falafels were king, really they were one of my absolute favorite nights out! Really nice and filling without feeling heavy, loaded with veggies, those mediterranean flavors just hit the spot.

INGREDIENTS:

1 - 2 Full Leaves Soft White or Red Cabbage
2 leaves Romaine Lettuce
2 roma tomatoes
1 Persian Cucumber
6 - 8 Falafel Balls (see recipe)

FILLING:
Falafel Balls
Tangy Tzatziki

PREPARATION:

Pick the most tender fresh cabbage possible, I love the big white cabbage leaves, great for wraps, burritos and falafels. Use one entire leaf for each 'pita', and prepare two. Shred the lettuce, slice the tomatoes and cucumbers into half rounds. You should already have the balls and sauce ready! Fill each cabbage leaf with a bed of shredded romaine, place 3-4 Falafel balls per "falafel", top with slices of tomatoes, cucumber and taziki to taste. Use optional sauces if desired and serve. So good. Served with tabouli is perfect!

TRA RETREAT TREATS
EAST INDIAN NIGHT

COCONUT MILK

COCO BUTTER VEGGIES

SAG VEGANEER

RAW EAST INDIAN 'RICE'

TRA RETREAT TREATS
COCONUT MILK

I love the simple flavor of homemade raw coconut milk. This base recipe can lead you to unlimited sauce variations that taste so so so authentic and amazing! Coconut milk in this simple form is the only food (beside breast milk) one can give a newborn baby with near zero chance of negative reaction, it's easy to digest and delicious!

INGREDIENTS:

1 mature brown Coconut

PREPARATION:

Using a corkscrew, screw into 2 of the 3 eyelets on the top of the coconut if possible, sometimes only one will go. Pour the water into the blender and place the coconut in a sturdy bag. Smash it on a cement floor or really hard surface until it breaks into multiple chunks. Using a spoon or carefully using a butter knife separate the hard white coconut from the shell and place into the blender. This can take some time, consider reserving ¼th the coconut for the rice recipe. The water should be at least ⅔ of the way covering the coconut, if not add some water. If you have a Vitamix simply blend at high speeds vigorously using the tamper to force the coconut into the blades till smooth, otherwise you may have to grate the coconut into the blender. Once smooth pour into a nutmilk bag or cheese cloth and strain. Whalla you have delicious coconut milk, usually 2- 3 cups worth enough for 2-4 servings. I usually use this much to make both the recipes below.

TRA RETREAT TREATS
COCOBUTTER VEGGIES

This is one of my favorite "Cravings Busters" raw dishes of all time! Creamy, flavorful and filling, when I discovered this and Sag Veganeer forgetting cooked east Indian food was a snap. Use the above coconut milk recipe and serve over the rice below.

INGREDIENTS:

1 ½ cups Coconut Milk
6 large Tomatoes (beefsteak or heirloom)
10 - 20 Crimini Mushrooms
½ a head Cauliflower
½ cup Sun-Dried Tomatoes,
2 Green Onions
1 bunch of Cilantro
1 thumb of Ginger

OPTIONAL
Garlic
Cumin/Turmeric/Chili Powder

PREPARATION:

Cut the top (stem end) ½ of the tomatoes off and place in the blender with coconut milk. Roughly chop the remaining bottom ½ of the tomatoes and place in a large bowl. Chop the mushrooms into 2 or 4 medium sized pieces add to the bowl. Roughly chop or break up the cauliflower and place in the bowl. Option to place all chopped ingredients on dehydrator trays and dehydrate for 2 hours at 109°, or in hot tap water (not mushrooms/chopped tomato in water) for 5 minutes, this softens everything and is really nice. Add sun dried tomatoes, green onion, cilantro, ginger and optional ingredients to the blender, blend till really smooth adding more sun dried tomatoes in needed to thicken. Pour over chopped veggies and mix well. Serve over "rice" and everything is nice!

TRA RETREAT TREATS
SAG VEGANEER

Another one of my favorite "Cravings Busters" raw dishes, this used to be my favorite East Indian dish and one I had a hard time letting go of. Simulating the "Sag" curried spinach and the "paneer", cheese, was a challenge but I actually think is much better tasting using the coconut milk recipe above and portobello mushrooms!

INGREDIENTS:

1 ½ cups Coconut Milk
1 ½ - 2 lbs. Baby Spinach
2 Portobello Mushrooms, cubed
2 Green Onions
1 thumb of Ginger

OPTIONAL
Garlic
Cumin
Turmeric
Masala (Cinnamon, Clove, Cardamom)

PREPARATION:

Put in a blender the coconut milk, portobello stems, green onion, ginger and optional ingredients, and blend until smooth. Place chopped mushrooms into a flat bottomed bowl and pour "broth" on top. Let sit to marinate 2 hours at room temperature. Strain broth back into the blender reserving the mushrooms in the bowl. Add ⅓ of the spinach to the blender and slowly pulse blend using a celery stick to force spinach into the blades (if using a vitamix, 6 on the speed dial using the tamper to push into the blades works perfect). With the vitamix it is easy to get 1 ½+ lbs. of spinach into the sauce using this technique, otherwise get all you can without fully pureeing the spinach. You should have about 1 ½ liters of "sag". Pour over the "Veganeer" mushroom cubes and mix well. Serve alone or with the cocobutter veggies n "rice!

TRA RETREAT TREATS
RAW EAST INDIAN "RICE"

A dozen ways to do this I will share using the most common Ingredients. In Costa Rica I love to use fresh heart of palm, in mexico jicama, At home my most common is made with cauliflower, but today we will use turnip, zucchini and coconut! Have fun with all the flavors n options, each brings a different flavor.

INGREDIENTS:

1 large Turnip
1 mediumZucchini
1 mature brown Coconut
Green Onion

OPTIONAL
dash of Turmeric

PREPARATION:

Peel the turnip and zucchini, using a medium fine grater, grate grate grate! Using a nutmilk bag, cheese cloth or colander and clean towel squeeze out some of the excess moisture, but not all. Add to a big bowl. If you reserved the ¼th of the coconut from the "coconut milk" recipe you're in luck, if not it's not vital. Using a fine grater grate the coconut into the bowl. Finely chop the green onion and add to the bowl along with the optional turmeric stirring and then fluffing. Simple simon! Cauliflower is often preferred – try it too – it makes more of a couscous-type rice. Easy to make with a food processor S-blade. Enjoy with the curry recipes on top!

TRA RETREAT TREATS
FAREWELL BREAKFAST

BANANA PANCAKES

BANANA FUDGE ICE CREAM

MANGO-DATE SYRUP

TRA RETREAT TREATS
BANANA PANCAKES

This is a really simple yet surprising recipe, really sweet and even fluffy like a regular pancake, a few with some banana Ice cream and your set! You can use regular bananas but I really prefer really ripe burro banana's. They are the shorter stubby ones that have a bit of a triangular shape instead of round, much denser than cavendish they make a thicker "batter".

INGREDIENTS:

13 Burro Bananas
¼ cup of Chia Seeds
Cinnamon, to taste

OPTIONAL
1 cup of Blueberries

PREPARATION:

If you can't find burro bananas Use 10 regular cavendish or 8 large soft black ripe plantains. Peel all bananas and blend with the chia seeds and cinnamon without using any water, use the tamper or blend in batches if needed. If using the blueberries pour the batter into a bowl and mix in the berries. Pour one pancake at a time onto teflex / parchment lined dehydrator sheets slowly trying to make as thick as possible (¼" - ½"). I find it easiest make 4 on each large excalibur tray, starting thick in the middle then circling the outside of the pancake to thicken the edges. A slight bit of touch ups with a chef knife or spoon if needed to smooth the top out or to bring a rough edge in.

Dehydrate at 109°F for 8 to 10 hours or until you can carefully peel the pancakes off the sheets. It helps to sandwich the pancakes between two sheets and slowly peel off the Teflex/Parchment paper. once flipped, continue dehydrating for 1 to 3 hours depending on the thickness. The center should be a little bit soft so that you can pick one up and it does not run or fall apart but you don't want if fully done like a "rollup".

Plate and serve with any banana Ice cream, fruit syrup (recipe below) and or any other sweet treats n greens! Should make 12+ pancakes... Enough to share!

TRA RETREAT TREATS
BANANA FUDGE ICE CREAM

Oh wow I used to love chocolate fudge ice cream, and now I still do!! I remember when I got a big stream of fudge I would rejoice, this recipe brings it all back, it's like mining for fudge in banana Ice cream ahaha. While we used negro sapote for the "fudge" at the retreat I will also give an alternative in the next recipe..

INGREDIENTS:

Ice Cream

8 Bananas, peeled and frozen

FUDGE OPTION 1

2 Black Sapote, de-seeded and frozen

1 - 2 tbs raw Carob powder

FUDGE OPTION 2

Fresh Ripe Banana, 1

Medjool Dates, 10

2 tbs raw Carob powder

PREPARATION:

Cut frozen bananas into loose chunks and blend in the Vitamix using the tamper vigorously, to keep the blender from heating up much (if necessary, split into two batches). Place in a casserole dish.

FUDGE OPTION 1

Loosely cut/scoop the frozen sapote and fold into the "banana Ice cream". Place back in the freezer for 30 minutes to harden, if necessary, serve with pancakes, fruit syrup or celery and bananas.

FUDGE OPTION 2

Peel and place banana in the Vitamix, pit dates and add them along with the carob powder to the blender. Blend well and pour into a small bowl. Place in freezer for 1 - 2 hours to harden. Loosely cut/scoop and fold into the "banana ice cream".

TRA RETREAT TREATS
MANGO-DATE SYRUP

Such an awesome, simple and versatile recipe we made at the retreat. It can also be used with any combination of dried and fresh fruit. This is my personal favorite, dates, mango juice and hot water. If you have dried fruit you can simply use more water for a thicker syrup.

INGREDIENTS:

6 Medjool Dates
2 Mangos
½ cup hot Water, or to desired consistency

PREPARATION:

Cut and blend the mango into a thick sauce, straining through a nutmilk bag, otherwise juice the mango. You should have 1 ½ cups. If you are not using a vitamix, pit and pre-soak the dates for 4 - 8 hours to soften, otherwise blend dates with the mango and then enough hot water to make a slightly runny sauce. Keep adding water if needed to desired consistency. You can just use more mango juice and no water if desired.

Serve over pancakes, crepes, dip for fruit sushi, pour over sliced bananas, shredded pears and apples... Limitless options!

HOT TIP:
Any dried fruit classifies as a sweet fruit for food combining! For example, date and dried pineapple go great together, or dried strawberries with raisins is superb!

TRA RETREAT TREATS
ABOUT THE HOSTS

MEGAN ELIZABETH MCDONNELL

CHRIS KENDALL

TRA RETREAT TREATS

MEGAN ELIZABETH MCDONNELL

PENNSYLVANIA, USA

Before following natural hygiene, Megan was struck with serious health issues in 2007 that changed her life forever. Her diet would be considered standard american for most of her life; although she was a vegetarian for several years. She had taken a few medications as a teenager for acne and anxiety, which was hard on the body and contributed to building the ill health she had experienced. Slightly overweight, misguided and uninformed about the pure path to health, as countless people find themselves, Megan sought solutions in many forms.

Her first book, Easy To Be Raw, is focused around sweet, fruit-based recipes which effortlessly bridged the gap between simple and gourmet; an important place in a raw food world which was otherwise left unfilled. She is most known for her successful books, Easy To Be Raw, and its follow-up, You in Bloom. These books in conjunction, available in paper and ebook format, have been written by her as "an open book" when it comes to sharing her tips, experiences, and of course, her recipes with those who seek it.

Megan can be found on her wildly popular YouTube Channel making recipes and sharing her outside-the-box lifestyle with all who are interested. She co-hosts and co-chefs at popular 80/10/10 North American raw food events. Her inspiring yet accessible perspective is contagious and joyful.

MEGAN'S MEDIA

Website: MeganElizabeth.com

Twitter: @WhatsUpMeganE

Facebook: MeganElizabethRaw

YouTube: EasyToBeRaw

TRA RETREAT TREATS
CHRIS KENDALL
SASKATCHEWAN, CANADA

Chris is a Registered Holistic Nutritionist (RHN), a lifelong athlete, creator of Kendalini Yoga, and a raw food lifestyle Coach. Since the age of 5 he has pushed his physical and mental boundaries athletically as a skateboarder and is still today a competitive raw vegan athlete and amateur skateboarder. Taking part in a period of poor lifestyle and food choices in his mid to late teens led to early injury, poor recovery, with a predictable decline in vitality, self esteem and vigour. It was these experiences that spawned a early interest in nutrition and its connection to fitness, self love and happiness by the age of 18.

Chris, aka The Banana Commander started his website and company The Raw Advantage in order to spread the word of the high energy holistic and raw food lifestyle. He is most known for his funky recipes, both quick and easy as well as being recognized as one of the première "transitional" and/or simple low-fat raw gourmet chefs in the world today. He can be found on his hugely popular and sometimes wild YouTube, Twitter, Facebook, Instagram and other social media sites tackling common raw food issues, sharing his life with people, answering holistic lifestyle questions and being a avid leader of the raw food movement. His combined young spirit and seasoned maturity is appealing to a wide fun-loving audience.

Lately, Chris can be found hosting all types of retreats, acting as lead chef, a speaker and yoga teacher at premier raw food events. His inspiring attitude, budding TRAdream charity and way of bringing ease to any situation will make you believe... anything is possible.

CK'S MEDIA

Website: TheRawAdvantage.com

Twitter: @TheRawAdvantage

Facebook: TRA.kendallchris

YouTube: Ck1NSH

Instagram: TheRawAdvantage

TRA RETREAT TREATS
ABOUT THE RETREAT CENTERS

CASA AXIS MUNDI

FINCA DA VIDA

TRA RETREAT TREATS
CASA AXIS MUNDI
YUCATÁN, MEXICO

Nestled in the heart of Yucatán, Mexico, Vallalolid has a true gem of a Raw Food and Vegan Bed and Breakfast called **Casa Axis Mundi**. "Axis Mundi" signifies the connection between sky and earth, where all four directions meet... A sacred place of healing and nurture, bringing higher and lower realms together to a still point of deep peace, harmony, and knowing.

Born from the inspiration and regeneration found within Paul and Beate Epp's own raw food Transformation, this center was created as a space and place to give back all the abundance they have received. Beate is a world famous Author, Reiki Master and raw food guide, all of which you can benefit from by simply being in her company and or asking for a treatment.

Settled in a peaceful and off the beaten path local mexican city, Casa Axis Mundi really has a lot of local flavour to offer within a walking distance. Cultural buildings, farmers markets, permaculture farms, parks, cenotes and ruins all add to amazing experience. The Casa itself really offers a pristine, magical space to read, go within, and expand within the centre itself. An amazing shared kitchen and dining area, large pool and sun deck, as well as exotic fruit trees are all on the path to your beautiful private suite.

I feel blessed to have been a small part of creative process as well as kicking off the grand opening of the Center with its first Retreat. I count Beate and Paul as close friends and feel so blessed to share their amazing essence and dream that is Casa Axis Mundi at yearly retreats.

For more info check **CasaAxisMundi.com**.

TRA RETREAT TREATS
FINCA DE VIDA
COSTA RICA

Finca de Vida or in English, Farm of Life, certainly lives up to its name. A amazing and vital organic farm, raw food healing and retreat center can be found in the amazingly lush tropical setting of Costa Rica. With every aspect of health covered, physical mental spiritual in various ways, this centre is sure to blow you away and leave you with seeds of growth and regeneration within.

The centers hosts, Brian and Jody Calvi both transformed their lives from a place of sickness and distress to ease and excitement via the raw food and holistic lifestyle. Developed with the key concept of affordability, Brian and Jody truly have created a Shangri-La. The Farm of Life is truly a space that anyone could come to, to simply relax, go on amazing Costa Rica Adventures and if desired learn the amazing healing properties of the human body when the precepts of nature are followed. WIth amazing all you can eat local fresh organic raw fruits and vegetables, 2 on-site pristine spring births, various fitness trails, a yoga hut on top of a mountainside, common area's as well as some of the most breathtaking views from each and every room they offer, I feel safe to say Fica de Vida is a premier raw food vacation destination. Both Brian and Jody are experienced health coaches offering various perusal skills and practices, from sun-gazing to yoga and chi gong... Sure to appease all.

I feel incredibly blessed to be a part of the Farm of Life Family and spend time every year with my hombre's at the Center for my own retreats and to simply love, live, laugh, and grow. Hope to see you there at my next retreat or as a Farm of Life Guest!

To learn more check FarmOfLifeCR.com .

THANKS
TRA RETREAT TREATS
FROM CK

More than blessed by the amazing Megan Elizabeth McDonnell as a co-host, adding her flare, expertise and fun. Thanks Megan for the help, inspiration, recipes and love added to the retreat, so excited for more! Check her out at **MeganElizabeth.com** and at **Megan's Youtube channel, EasyToBeRaw.**

Honored by the amazing retreat attendees at both retreat centers, thanks so much for enjoying, opening up, connecting and growing together. Times we will never forget, this book commemorating the experience! SO excited for all future retreats :)

Thousand Thanks to Paul and Beate Epp, of **Casa Axis Mundi** for creating and sharing their dream. I am so excited to be a part of their budding center.

Endless gratitude and thanks to Brian and Josephine Calvi of **Finca de Vida** and to Team Awesome (of which I'm a part). I feel so blessed to come to the Farm of Life Year after year, growing living laughing and flowing with the Farm of Life family and the farm itself. SO much more to come there!

Always much much Thanks to Dr. Douglas Graham for Pointing to the moon, I feel blessed by your mentorship, friendship and sharing. For top notch info, books, retreats and much much more, peep everything he has to offer at FoodnSport.com. And PS: If you haven't, check out The 80/10/10 Diet, **available at TheRawAdvantage.com**, or at **FoodnSport.com.**

TRA RETREAT TREATS
THANKS

Big thanks to **Adam Berry**, **Emma Sabourin**, and **Megan Elizabeth** for epic pictures and times shared.

So blessed by Ryan Lewis of **Canistel Design** for really helping me out in a tight and tough spot. He has come through with amazing editing, formatting, and graphic design on this book as well as on my **new website**. I am really excited to see TRA flow and grow with him and his artistic vision.

I feel so so blessed to connect with others, spreading the seeds of health creation and thus self love within all. The path of self improvement isn't always easy, It seldom comes without some bumps and stretching of one's comfort zone. It's those experiences that we grow most, together we can open our hearts and minds to the true ease and bliss that comes with being in line with natures design. Spreading my passion for health and fitness in beautiful places brings me so much joy that I can surely say there will be many more retreats to come.

From Mexico to Costa Rica, to unlimited potentials in Hawaii, Canada, Asia, Europe and Beyond.. Stay in touch to grow with me :)

More information on TRA Retreats and
3 free ebooks await you at TheRawAdvantage.com!

Made in the USA
Monee, IL
03 October 2020